STEAM
TRAINS

STEAM TRAINS

BERNARD FITZSIMONS

CHARTWELL BOOKS, INC.

© 1982 Winchmore Publishing Services Ltd.

ISBN 0-89009-513-2

First published in the United States of America by:
Chartwell Books Inc.
A Division of Book Sales Inc.
110 Enterprise Avenue
Secaucas, New Jersey 07094

Produced by Winchmore Publishing Services Limited
48 Lancaster Avenue
Hadley Wood
Herts.

Designed by Andrzej Bielecki
Edited by Sue Butterworth

Printed in Hong Kong

Color Separation by
Capricorn Reproductions, London.

Santa Fe class 2900
locomotive No. 2925

CONTENTS

STEAM AND THE RAILWAYS

THE OBVIOUS ADVANTAGES to be gained by running wheeled vehicles, especially those carrying heavy loads, on relatively smooth rails rather than rough and uneven ground, have been appreciated for many centuries. As early as 1550 illustrations appeared of wagonways used in German mines, and over the next 200 years their use became common in mines all over Europe. In Britain, especially, they were used to ferry coal from the mines to nearby rivers and, later, to the canals.

For many years only wooden rails were used, and the wheels of the wagons had grooved or flanged rims for guidance. Later, iron plating was added to prolong the life of the rails, and towards the end of the eighteenth century cast iron plates, usually laid on stone blocks and formed with flanges to guide plain wheels, became more common.

At the same time, other operators began to experiment with iron rails, rather than plates, which were intended for use with flanged wheels. The next step was the introduction of wrought iron, which enabled much longer rails to be used, and in 1820 a system of rolling lengths of wrought iron of uniform cross-section was patented. Ultimately, the modern forms of railway track were evolved, but in the meantime another line of development was under way that would both cement the railways' relationship with coal and at the same time allow their use to be extended far beyond the pitheads and coal wharves where they originated.

The plateways and railways built up to the end of the eighteenth century were generally private concerns, built and operated by the owners of the mines which they served. And although there were fairly extensive networks in some areas, notably around the Tyne and Wear rivers in north-east England, long-distance transport remained the preserve of the waterways.

The construction of canals where navigable rivers did not exist was an expensive business, and by the beginning of the nineteenth century there were numerous schemes for long-distance railways. In 1801 a significant step was taken when the Surrey Iron Railway was authorized by Act of Parliament to carry public traffic over the nine miles (14·5 km) between Croydon and the River Thames at Wandsworth, and in 1803 it opened as the first officially sanctioned public railway.

However, as long as the wagons were drawn by horses there were practical limits on the weight and speed of traffic that railways could carry. The steam engines that were becoming increasingly common by the end of the eighteenth century seemed to offer a promising source of power and as early as 1769 Nicolas Cugnot had built a steam carriage in Paris, only to be imprisoned for his pains. By the time the Surrey Iron Railway was opened in 1803, an English engineer, Richard Trevithick, had produced his first steam-propelled vehicle for use on the roads.

Trevithick was the son of a mine engineer in Cornwall, and in 1801, using his experience with steam pumping engines in the local mineral mines, he built a successful steam carriage which incorporated a return

Wooden trucks on the wagonway at the head of the Derby Canal and Little Eaton

flue to heat the water in the boiler. A second steam carriage was followed by a locomotive designed to run on the plateway between the Penydaren Ironworks, in South Wales, and a local canal. It is ironic that such an epochal machine should have been made purely to settle a substantial wager between the owner of the ironworks and a competitor, but on 21 February 1804, the bet was won: Trevithick's locomotive easily hauled the specified ten tons of iron, augmented by a number of passengers, the length of the ten-mile (16·1 km) plateway, though only at the cost of heavy damage to the iron plates.

This pioneer locomotive employed a single horizontal cylinder, with a large flywheel, and the wheels were driven through a system of gears, while his *Catch-me-who-can* of 1808 used a vertical cylinder to drive the wheels by means of connecting rods, but after a demonstration in London failed to attract any backing Trevithick abandoned steam engines to look for gold in South America.

In 1805, however, he had built another engine for the Wylam colliery, which operated one of the wagonways on the banks of the Tyne. This engine, like the Peny-daren model, proved too heavy for the plateway, but it inspired a number of local engineers to build their own experimental locomotives. The most important of these was George Stephenson.

Although barely literate, Stephenson was both a mechanical genius and a visionary, who not only perfected the basic pattern on which all steam loco-motives were based, but also foresaw the creation of a national railway network. Each of Stephenson's locomotives embodied further improvements on Trevithick's original pattern: his first, the *Blucher*, of 1814, had flanged wheels to run on rails rather than plates, and in subsequent engines he perfected a direct drive from the cylinders via connecting rods to the driving wheels. When he became involved in the planning of the Stockton and Darlington Railway,

Stephenson adopted wrought iron I-section rails, mounted in chairs on the stone blocks to provide continuity in the joints, and his first locomotive for the new railway, the *Locomotion*, used rods rather than chains to connect the two pairs of wheels.

The opening of the Stockton and Darlington Rail-way on 27 September 1825 was a historic occasion, marking the first use of steam power on a public railway, but the locomotives were still prone to boiler explosions and broken wheels. By this time George Stephenson had become the acknowledged expert on railways and locomotives, and he was invited to advise on the construction and operation of a project-ed railway between Liverpool and Manchester. The mixed results achieved on the Stockton and Darling-ton, where substantial savings in operating costs were offset by the persistent unreliability of the locomotives, left the directors of the new company unconvinced that steam locomotives should be adopted. Horses, or

Previous page: The wagonway from the head of the Derby canal at Little Eaton to Denby colliery was built in the 1790s and in use until 1908

Below: Richard Trevithick's last locomotive, *Catch-me-who-can*, on exhibition in London in 1808

Right: Before the directors of the Liverpool and Manchester Railway would accept steam locomotives a series of trials were held in 1829

Far right: A replica of Stephenson's *Rocket* is demonstrated in London's Hyde Park in 1979

stationary engines hauling the trains by cable, were suggested as alternatives, and to settle the question a series of trials were held in October 1829.

The undoubted star of the contest was the *Rocket*, built by the firm which George Stephenson had founded and of which his son Robert was the head. The essential features of the *Rocket* which endured throughout the development of the steam locomotive were the multitube boiler and the blast pipe. Hot gases from the fire passed through the firetubes in the boiler, heating the water to produce steam. The steam was fed to the cylinders, where by acting on the pistons it drove the wheels, and was then exhausted through a blast pipe in the chimney to create the draught on the fire.

By the time the Liverpool and Manchester Railway was ready to begin operations in September 1830, news of the new steam railways was creating widespread interest. Across the Atlantic, where settlement

of the fertile river valleys in the interior of the United States was getting under way, there was a desperate need for improved communications. The new government roads enabled settlers to reach the rivers of the interior, and the Erie canal provided an additional waterway for grain exports, which otherwise were shipped south down the Mississippi to New Orleans.

The response of the east coast cities, once New York had secured the first water route to the Great Lakes, was to seek their own means of communications, and with the mountain ranges forming a formidable obstacle to new canals, a number of them turned to railways as a possible solution.

First in the race was Baltimore, and in February 1828 the Maryland state legislature chartered the Baltimore and Ohio Railroad, an ambitious scheme for a 380 mile (611·8 km) railway that would connect with the Ohio River at Wheeling. Work was begun on 4 July 1829, and by the following year

horses were hauling rail cars over the first 13 miles (20·9 km) of track.

Already, a steam locomotive had been tested in the United States: the Delaware and Hudson Canal company had sent Horatio Allen to observe the Rainhill trials, and he had ordered four locomotives, one from Robert Stephenson and the rest from the Stourbridge firm of Foster, Rastrick. It was one of the latter, the *Stourbridge Lion*, which on 8 August 1829, made the first steam locomotive trip in America, and a year later the *Tom Thumb*, built by one of the Baltimore and Ohio shareholders, Peter Cooper, was tested on the B&O's track between Baltimore and Ellicott's Mills.

On 28 August, *Tom Thumb* pulled a coach carrying 36 passengers at speeds of up to 18 mph (29 kmh), and when a horse-drawn car challenged Cooper to a race, the locomotive proved easily the faster, before the belt driving the fan that provided the draught for the

Below: An early train on the Liverpool and Manchester Railway crosses the Sankey viaduct, showing the rapid development of civil engineering that the railways inspired

Left: A 1927 replica of the Baltimore and Ohio Railroad's locomotive *Atlantic*, the first of the 'grasshopper' engines built by Phineas Davis after his prototype *York* had won the competition in 1831

Below left: The first stone was laid on the Baltimore and Ohio Railroad, America's pioneer railway, on 4 July 1828

fire slipped out of place and halted the steam engine.

Nevertheless, Cooper had proved his point, and the railroad offered prizes for the best locomotives to be entered in a competition held on 1 June 1831. The only locomotive able to meet the conditions of the competition was the *York*, built by Phineas Davis, and as a result the Baltimore and Ohio ordered 20 further examples of Davis' 'grasshopper' engines. The first of these was named *Atlantic*, and several of the class served the railroad for over 50 years.

By this time other cities had followed Baltimore's lead, and railroads were being built westwards from Boston, Philadelphia, Richmond, Charleston and Savannah. Within a few years others were started to connect the inland cities with the lakes, rivers and seas that still formed the main long-distance transport routes, and new firms were building locomotives to operate them. By the middle of the nineteenth century the United States would have the biggest rail network in the world, and the railways would go on to transform the republic, but in the meantime the more industrialized nations of Europe were able to make better progress with the development of the railways.

The first railway in France was opened between Andrezieux and St Etienne in 1828, though steam traction was not introduced until 1832 on a new line from St Etienne to Lyons. New lines followed in Germany and Belgium in 1835, and by the end of the decade steam railways were in operation in Ireland, Austria, the Netherlands and Italy. Other countries followed suit during the 1840s, and while these usually relied on locomotives built by Stephenson or other English constructors to begin with, national characteristics soon became apparent as indigenous designs were produced.

One consequence of the initial use of Stephenson locomotives, however, was the widespread adoption of Stephenson's 'standard' gauge, or distance between the rails, of 4 ft $8\frac{1}{2}$ in (143·5 cm). This was selected in the first place for no better reason than it happened to be the gauge used on the mine railway where Stephenson's first experiments were carried out, but ultimately the benefits of uniformity outweighed the drawbacks of the restricted width, and only Russia, Finland, Spain and Portugal chose different gauges. Consequently, it was soon possible to run international trains through most of Europe.

Another characteristic of the continental railways was the large measure of government control that was exercised over their location. In the United States and Britain many competing lines were built, and it was many years before even the gauge was standardized on a national basis. Elsewhere in Europe, on the other hand, the tendency was for the national governments to license private companies to build along selected routes, or to undertake the construction themselves, thus avoiding a good deal of the wasteful competition that was to mar the development of the British and American systems.

Background: Johann Schubert's *Saxonia*, the first successful locomotive built in Germany, hauls the inaugural train on the Leipzig-Dresden railway in April 1839. Also shown is the original station at Leipzig

Left: The 2–4–0 tank engine *Licaon*, one of a class built for the Austrian Northern Railway 1848–53

Right: The Stephenson locomotive *Der Adler* worked the first Swiss railway, between Zurich and Baden, from 1847

Far right: Locomotive No 13 of the Dutch state railway, built in 1864 by the English firm of Beyer, Peacock

GROWTH OF THE NETWORKS

WHILE CONTINENTAL RAILWAYS were making cautious progress and American builders were struggling with the lack of an industrial base in their efforts to bridge the huge distances between coastal ports and inland waterways, the success of the Liverpool and Manchester venture sparked off almost unbounded enthusiasm for new lines in Britain.

Even before the Liverpool and Manchester was opened, various connecting lines were being promoted, and the Stephensons found themselves in great demand. Of course, there was opposition from the canal owners who saw their livelihoods threatened, and from landowners who wanted no part of the new mode of transport, and Parliamentary approval was required for any new railway. But the march of progress proved irresistible, and within a few years new lines were being planned, built and opened all over the country.

In 1837 the Grand Junction Railway was opened between Warrington and Birmingham to complete the first trunk route between the latter city and Liverpool and Manchester. And while George Stephenson was engaged on the Grand Junction, his son, Robert, was at work on a route from Birmingham to London.

The London and Birmingham Railway faced particularly fierce opposition. The original bill to authorize its construction was heavily defeated in 1831, but after agreement had been reached with the landowners affected on an appropriate price for right of way a new bill was passed without particular opposition two years later. It then remained to build the line, and despite formidable obstacles requiring un-

precedented feats of civil engineering, not least in the approaches to the London terminus at Euston, the new railway was opened in 1838.

All the lines in which the Stephensons were involved were built to the standard gauge of 4 ft 8½ in (143·5 cm) which they had inherited from the Killingworth colliery wagonway, and while the benefits of uniformity became increasingly apparent as new lines began to intersect, not everyone was convinced of its advantages. One of its most stubborn opponents was Robert Stephenson's only real rival as the greatest engineer of the day, Isambard Kingdom Brunel.

Like Stephenson, Brunel was the son of another eminent engineer; like him, too, he began his career early and successfully, and in 1833, at the age of 27, he was appointed engineer of the Great Western Railway, planned to connect London and Bristol. In common with the other new railways, the Great Western was opposed by powerful interests inside and outside Parliament, but in 1835 approval was secured and work was started.

For the main line to Bristol, Brunel had selected a route via Swindon that offered the minimum possible gradients and curves, and with the intention of operating the trains at the highest possible speeds he recommended that the track should be constructed to a gauge of seven feet (213·4 cm) between the rails. His reasoning in arriving at this gauge was not entirely flawless, though there were undoubted advantages to be gained, but Brunel convinced the directors, and the broad gauge was adopted.

Having begun with an entirely new gauge, Brunel went on to depart from established practice in almost every aspect of his work. To support the rails, which themselves were formed with a bridge-shaped section, he used longitudinal timbers, braced by cross-ties and supported on timber piles sunk in the earth. His bridge over the Thames at Maidenhead was designed with brick arches so flat that its design was criticized widely, though erroneously, as impractical; his Box Tunnel, near Bath, was easily the longest of its day; and for the South Devon Railway, between Exeter and Plymouth, he introduced the atmospheric system of operation, which used stationary pumps to evacuate a length of pipe and effectively suck a connected locomotive along the line.

In many of his ideas Brunel was simply wrong: the rigidity of his permanent way proved to be a drawback rather than an advantage, and the atmospheric system had to be abandoned after a short period. On the other hand, with the singular exception of locomotives, Brunel made notable contributions to every aspect of the Great Western's operations, and his stations, bridges and other structures helped set a

style that made his railway the most glamorous of all the British main lines.

Ultimately, the broad gauge itself had to go, not because of any inherent defect, but because the spreading railway network made the transfers between standard and broad gauge lines anachronistic: one or the other had to be made universal, and in the end the simple fact that standard gauge trains could run through broad gauge stations and other structures, while the reverse was impossible, made the retention of the standard gauge inevitable. The first conversion of a broad guage line was made in 1869, and in 1892 the work was completed.

By the end of the nineteenth century, the majority of the small lines that had appeared early in the development of the railway system had been consolidated into a number of large companies. All of these developed their own characteristic styles, which were reflected in the architecture of their stations, the pattern of their services and, most immediately, in the brightly painted locomotives which they operated.

Naturally, there were discernible general trends. The track itself in the mid-Victorian period placed limitations on the weight of both locomotives and trains, and single driving wheels of large diameter became common on the fastest passenger engines. Perhaps the most famous examples were the 4-2-2s with 8 ft (243·8 cm) diameter driving wheels built by Patrick Stirling for the Great Northern Railway. Developed over a period of 25 years from their introduction in 1870, these engines worked the fastest passenger services in the world during the 1880s.

For general service, four driving wheels gave greater adhesion with the firebox carried between the driving axles, and 2-4-0s were commonly used, though a few designers preferred to have the driving wheels in front, and some outstanding 0-4-2s were used by the London, Brighton and South Coast Railway. Towards the end of the Victorian era four-coupled engines with leading bogies were adopted by many railways, and the last years of the nineteenth century saw the appearance of the first British Atlantic type 4-4-2s.

During this period a degree of competition developed between some of the leading companies. British express services were easily the fastest in the world during the 1880s, though trains were relatively light and sustained speeds of 40-50 mph (64·4-80·5 kmh) rather than really high maximum speeds were the rule. The introduction of bogie passenger carriages during the 1870s enabled a new level of comfort to be provided, and together with the adoption of continuous brakes, block signalling and other safety measures permitted considerably higher speeds. Improved track also encouraged faster running, and towards the end of the 1880s there were the first signs of an acceleration in scheduled services.

The premier long-distance routes were those from London to Edinburgh. Up the east coast, services

Left: Building a cutting on the London and Birmingham Railway's approach to Euston

Top left: The English entrance to the Great Western Railway's Severn tunnel

15

Left: The Liverpool and Manchester Railway's locomotive *Lion* was restored to working order after a career as a pumping engine in Liverpool docks

Right: The Great Western Railway's Temple Meads station at Bristol was begun by Brunel in the 1830s, and the last of a series of additions was completed in 1935

Below: The London, Brighton and South Coast Railway's Gladstone class 0–4–2, first built in 1882, was unusual in having the coupled driving wheels at the front

were operated by the Great Northern and North Eastern railways, while the London and North Western and Caledonian railways ran the competing service over the slightly longer west coast route. In 1888 an initial acceleration by the Great Northern and North Eastern was ended by agreement with the west coast companies, and standard timings of eight hours by the west coast route, and a quarter of an hour less on the shorter east coast lines were agreed.

However, within five years timetables were being adjusted again. The opening of the Forth Bridge in 1889 gave the east coast companies a direct line, in conjunction with the North British Railway, to Aberdeen, and in July 1895 a period of open racing began on the two main lines.

At the start of the racing, the fastest journey was at an average speed of just over 45 mph (72·4 kmh), but by 20 August, with the east coast companies pro-

gressively tightening their schedules and the west coast rivals simply running a special high-speed section of the train flat out, average speeds close to 60 mph (96·6 kmh) were being achieved.

On 21 August the east coast lines pushed the speed to an average of 60·6 mph (97·6 kmh) using one of the Great Northern's Stirling eight-foot (243·8 cm) singles between Kings Cross and York, and North Eastern and North British 4–4–0s for the remainder of the journey. The following night the west coast companies replied with a time of only 512 minutes for the 540 mile (869·4 km) trip for a record average speed of $63\frac{1}{4}$ mph (101·8 kmh). The engines involved in this achievement were a three-cylinder compound 4–4–0 between Euston and Crewe and the Precedent class 2–4–0 *Hardwicke* from Crewe to Carlisle, followed by Caldeonian Railway 4–4–0s for the rest of the run to Aberdeen.

Below left: Patrick Stirling's locomotive No 1 for the Great Northern Railway was built in 1870 with 8 ft (243·8 cm) diameter driving wheels for high-speed traffic

Bottom left: The impressive curve of York station, built in the 1870s, was adopted to effect a junction between the termini of the two railways serving the city, the Great Northern and the North Eastern

Below: Locomotives with single driving wheels were given a new lease of life in the late Victorian era with the introduction of steam sanding gear, but the increasing weight of trains had made them obsolete by the end of the nineteenth century. This example is one of the single-wheelers built by Samuel Johnson for the Midland Railway from 1887

Overleaf: *Hardwicke*, the London and North Western Railway's Precedent class locomotive which helped set the record for the fastest service between London and Aberdeen in 1895

The star of the west coast effort was the *Hardwicke*, which covered the 141 miles (227 km) between Crewe and Carlisle in only 126 minutes, at an average speed of 67·2 mph (108·2 kmh) and including the steep climb over Shap Fell. But such times were not repeated: a series of derailments and the growing weight of trains placed the accent on the ability to haul bigger trains rather than reach the highest speeds, and it was not until the 1930s that all-out speeding reappeared on the routes to Scotland.

Meanwhile, the development of railways in the United States had followed a radically different course from that in Britain. Despite some early setbacks they continued to spread, and by 1850 there were some 9,000 miles (14,490 km) of railway in operation. Another decade saw that total more than trebled, but the 1860s brought civil war and a temporary setback to new construction.

The fighting between Union and Confederate armies saw much destruction of the railways in the areas of conflict. At the same time, the unprecedented demand for transport of men and supplies over vast distances gave an enormous stimulus to the northern network, augmented by the efforts of the United States Military Railroads which were formed as part of the Union war effort. By the time the war ended in 1865 the U.S.M.R.R. was operating more than 400 locomotives and 6,000 cars and controlled over 2,000 miles (3,220 km) of track, and had been responsible for the repair of many bridges and sections of track that had been destroyed by enemy action.

The most significant wartime development, however, was the chartering of the first transcontinental railway, a move that had been advocated widely before the war but had been given added importance by the need to unite the new settlements of the west

BRITISH STEAM IN THE TWENTIETH CENTURY

THE EARLY YEARS of the twentieth century were a period of growth and prosperity for British railways. Numbers of passengers booked increased steadily – the figures for the Midland Railway's St Pancras station show an annual rise from 650,000 in 1900 to 880,000 in 1913 – and with the network substantially complete the leading companies concentrated their efforts on operating trains of growing weight and improved comfort.

The crowded main lines did not encourage the highest speeds, and there was only one instance of the kind of all-out racing that had occurred on the Scottish routes in 1895. This took place on the Great Western and London and South Western lines between Plymouth and London with the ocean mail traffic in 1904.

An agreement between the two companies gave the Great Western the responsibility for carrying the mails to London, while passengers travelled by the London and South Western, but both companies were aware of the prestige value of making the fastest journey. In 1903 the Great Western had established a record of $233\frac{1}{2}$ minutes for the 246·6 miles (397 km) between Plymouth and Paddington, and in April 1904 a new sereies of races began. The climax came the following month, on 9 May, when the City class 4–4–0 *City of Truro* passed 100 mph (161 kmh) with an Ocean Mail special.

These record runs were made with lightweight special trains, but the Great Western also boasted the fastest scheduled services in the world. In 1902 daily services were run between London and Birmingham at $55\frac{1}{2}$ mph (89·4 kmh), in 1903 the fastest services on the run to Bristol were scheduled at just under 60 mph (96·6 kmh) and in 1904 the *City of Truro* inaugurated the Cornish Riviera Express, the longest non-stop run in the world, which averaged $55\frac{1}{2}$ mph (89·4 kmh) for the $245\frac{1}{2}$ mile (395·3 km) journey.

The growing weight of these fast services called for more powerful locomotives, and the logical step was to add a third pair of driving wheels. This solution was adopted by most of the main-line companies before the First World War, most successfully on the Great Western in the form of the series of 4–6–0s designed by George Churchward.

Churchward studied contemporary practice on foreign railways, and in his prototype No 98 of 1903 he combined a new type of tapered boiler with the continental Belpaire firebox, the American style of outside cylinders and cylinders and valve gear that allowed the freest passage of steam and used long-stroke pistons that would use it most efficiently. The subsequent two-cylinder Saint and four-cylinder Star classes were outstanding engines, and after his retirement in 1921 the Star type was developed into the famous Castle class.

The first of the Castles, *Caerphilly Castle*, appeared in 1923, and the type proved so successful that modified versions were still being built in 1950. Among the notable achievements of the Castles in service was the record-breaking run with the Cheltenham Flyer in June 1932, when the 77 miles (124 km) between Swindon and Paddington were covered at an average speed of 81·7 mph (132 kmh).

By the time the Castles appeared, of course, a wholesale reorganization of the British railway companies had taken place. During the First World War the railways had been brought under government control, and afterwards there were moves to nationalize them, but in the face of opposition from the companies a policy of compulsory amalgamation was substituted.

A total of 120 companies were formed into four main groups, of which the Great Western was the only one to retain its original name. The other new groups were the London, Midland and Scottish, which included the London and North Western, Midland and Caledonian among its major con-

Below: The preserved Great Western Railway locomotive *Clun Castle*, one of the outstanding Castle class four-cylinder 4–6–0s introduced in 1923 and produced in modified versions until 1951

Bottom: Passengers boarding the GWR Cornish Riviera Express at Paddington station in 1912

Bottom: The preserved Southern Railway four-cylinder 4–6–0 *Lord Nelson*, built in 1926 for high-speed working with the heaviest expresses, under steam in 1981 near Ribblehead. The *Lord Nelson* class locomotives were rebuilt with new cylinders and blast pipes by Oliver Bulleid

stituents; the London and North Eastern, which included the North Eastern, Great Northern and Great Eastern; and the Southern, which united the London and South Western with the other companies serving the south coast.

In the aftermath of the amalgamation, Churchward's influence began to make itself felt outside the Great Western. On the Southern Railway, for example, the King Arthur class 4–6–0s inherited from the London and South Western were not capable of meeting 55 mph (88·6 kmh) schedules with the 500-ton (508-tonne) trains that were becoming necessary to meet the demands of traffic. The four-cylinder 4–6–0s of the Lord Nelson class which were provided to deal with the heaviest expresses were designed after studies of the Castle class, though the actual layout of the cylinders, with all four in line, differed from that of the Castles, which had the outside cylinders set back so that connecting rods of equal length could be used.

The London, Midland and Scottish also benefited from Churchward's influence when William Stanier,

An example of one of the
most versatile of all British
locomotive types, the
London, Midland and
Scottish Railway's Class 5
'Black Five', leaving
Bournemouth for York in
1966

The DEVON BELLE

Fridays, Saturdays, Sundays and Mondays in each direction

dep 12.0 noon	Waterloo	arr 5.20 pm
arr 3.16 pm	Sidmouth Jct.	dep 2.3 pm
arr 3.36 pm	Exeter Ctl.	dep 1.40 pm
arr 5.32 pm	Ilfracombe	dep 12.0 noon
arr 5.36 pm	Plymouth Friary	dep 11.30 am

NEW!

ALL-PULLMAN TRAIN TO THE WEST OF ENGLAND
with Observation Car

SOUTHERN RAILWAY & PULLMAN CAR COMPANY

who had previously been employed by the Great Western, became chief mechanical engineer. Among the designs produced by Stanier were the Black Five 4–6–0s, of which no fewer than 842 were built between 1934 and 1951, and which proved capable of virtually any type of work.

Meanwhile, the trend in the biggest passenger engines had been towards the Pacific type, whose pair of rear carrying wheels allowed a bigger firebox to be used. The first British Pacific had been produced by Churchward in 1908, but this example, the *Great Bear*, proved too big and heavy for most of the Great Western's lines, and no more Pacifics were built in Britain until after the grouping.

In 1922, however, the London and North Eastern Railway produced two types: the 1921 Railways Act which enforced the grouping allowed the companies a period of preliminary organization, and the new organization did not take effect until the beginning of 1923. Consequently, both the North Eastern and

the Great Northern were able to produce their own designs, the former by Sir Vincent Raven and the latter by Nigel Gresley. Gresley became chief mechanical engineer of the new group, and while only five of the Raven Pacifics were built, his own prototypes formed the basis of an impressive series.

Again, the Castles had an influence on the new design: comparative trials between the two types in 1925 convinced Gresley that the higher boiler pressure employed in the Churchward design was worthwhile in terms of economical working. Accordingly, in 1928 production of the A3 Pacifics began.

The new engines were spectacularly successful. In March 1935, on a special trial run between Kings Cross and Newcastle-upon-Tyne, the A3 *Papyrus* covered well over half the 537-mile (864·6-km) round trip at 80 mph (128·8 kmh), reaching a maximum speed of 108 mph (173·9 kmh) and recording an average of 69·8 mph (112·3 kmh) for the return trip from Newcastle.

It was then decided to institute a four-hour schedule for the Newcastle service, and in order to ensure this could be achieved in normal traffic a new design of Pacific, the A4, was ordered. The first of the new engines, *Silver Link*, made its public debut on a special trial in September 1935, and more records were broken, with a top speed of $112\frac{1}{2}$ mph (181·1 kmh) being recorded.

To go with the specially streamlined A4s, new trains of streamlined stock were produced for the four-hour Silver Jubilee service. By this stage, the London and North Eastern and London, Midland and Scottish had become involved in a new version of the 1895 races to Scotland, the agreement that had ended those contests having been abandoned in 1932.

In 1933, the L.M.S.R. introduced the new Princess class Pacifics for the Royal Scot service between London and Glasgow, and following the introduction of the streamlined Silver Jubilee train the company set about producing its own streamlined Pacifics. The first of the new engines were built for a new service inaugurated in 1937 and named the Coronation Scot, which was scheduled to cover the 401 miles (645·6 km) between London and Glasgow in $6\frac{1}{2}$ hours.

By this time, the London and North Eastern had introduced a six-hour service between London and Edinburgh, the Coronation, which involved speeds of 100 mph (161 kmh) on many occasions, and in 1938, under the pretext of carrying out braking trials an all-out attempt was made at a new speed record. The engine was the A4 Pacific *Mallard*, and on 3 July a speed of 126 mph (202·9 kmh) was reached with the Silver Jubilee train and a special dynamometer car to record the performance. The record was established only at the cost of severe overheating, and the following year the Second World War intervened to put a stop to any further attempts at increased speeds on the Scottish services.

The achievements of the streamlined Pacifics could not fail to influence other designers. One who was particularly open to such influence was Oliver Bulleid, who, as Gresley's assistant, had been closely involved in the evolution of the A4's streamlined form.

Streamlined A4 Pacifics

Left: No 60024 *Kingfisher* at Perth in 1965

Top: No 60022 *Mallard*, the world speed record holder, with the down Tyne-Tees Pullman at Potters Bar

Below: No 60027 with the up Elizabethan at Potters Bar in December 1949

Right: No 60031 with an excursion train in Scotland in November 1965

Below right: No 4498 towing Great Northern No 1 at Shildon, during the celebrations held in August 1975 to celebrate the 150th anniversary of the Stockton and Darlington Railway

Left: Rebuilt Southern Railway Merchant Navy class Pacific No 35008 *Orient Line* at Southampton with the London-Weymouth boat train in January 1966

Below: West Country class Pacific No 123 *Blackmoor Vale* double-headed with a C class 0–6–0 on the Bluebell Line in May 1976

In 1937 Bulleid became chief mechanical engineer on the Southern Railway, which had for some years been engaged in electrifying sections of its main line. Bulleid's first move was to improve many members of the existing Lord Nelson, King Arthur and Schools classes by the addition of Lemaitre multiple blast pipes.

In his original designs, Bulleid showed a tendency to innovation on a comprehensive scale. The most obvious feature of his Merchant Navy class Pacifics, which first appeared in 1941, was the 'air-smoothed' casing, but along with the striking exterior came a wealth of novel details. The valve gear was enclosed in an oil bath, the firebox and high-pressure boiler, which tapered underneath to accommodate the inside cylinder, were of welded steel, and the wheels were an adaptation of the American 'Boxpok' type, while minor features included electric lighting and steam-powered firedoors.

Many of the design points of the Merchant Navy class were intended to simplify production in war conditions, but the overall purpose was to enable average speeds of up to 70 mph (112·7 kmh) to be maintained with 600-ton (610-tonne) trains. By the end of the war a lighter version, the West Country class, was being produced, to be followed by a further series of the Battle of Britain class, 80 of the total of 140 air-smoothed Pacifics being of the two later series.

By 1949 Bulleid had gone even further with his experiments in the form of the Leader class prototype, which was carried on two six-wheel powered bogies and featured a cab at each end with a central compartment for the fireman. The Leader class never progressed beyond the single example, and after Bulleid's retirement many of his Pacifics were rebuilt. The casing was removed, conventional valve gear substituted and the oil bath dispensed with, while the Leader was scrapped.

Bulleid's departure from the Southern Railway was preceded, at the beginning of 1948, by the nationalization of British Railways. Administration was divided into six regions, corresponding to the four groups formed after the First World War but with the separation of the lines in Scotland and of the southern section of the L.N.E.R. to form new Scottish and Eastern regions.

Provision of locomotives for the newly nationalized railways was placed in the hands of the Locomotive Standards Committee, and as a first move a series of trials of the locomotives of the various companies was held in 1948. The criteria for new designs established as a result included the maximization of steam-raising capacity, versatility in service, simplicity of maintenance and efficiency of the various components. And to ensure the highest possible degree of standardization, the design work was divided between the offices of the four old groups.

Initially, ten standard designs were evolved to replace the 400 types then in service, of which six were

Left: The last steam locomotive built for British Railways, the Class 9 2–10–0 *Evening Star*, under steam at York station in November 1976

Below: Britannia class Pacific No 70006 climbing Shap with a Blackpool-Glasgow train

to be built from the start with the others being kept in reserve. At the same time, passenger coaches and freight wagons were to be standardized.

The first of the new designs to appear was the most powerful of the new classes, the Pacific No 7000 *Britannia* being the first example. These Class 7 locomotives were, two-cylinder engines of straightforward construction embodying what were considered to be the most suitable of the components used by the old groups.

Hardly had production of the first series of standard types got under way, however, when the decision was taken to end production of steam locomotives altogether. The plan to begin conversion to diesel traction was announced in 1955, and by 1960 the construction of steam locomotives was at an end.

The last steam engine built for British Railways, the appropriately named *Evening Star*, was a member of the Class 9 2–10–0 heavy freight series. Although designed for maximum power, the Class 9 was also intended for use on mixed services, and in the event proved so versatile that it was capable of speeds of 90 mph (144·9 kmh), one example being used in an emergency to haul the Flying Scotsman.

Ten years after the announcement of the modernization plan, on 11 November 1965, the last regular steam-hauled passenger train left Paddington, and three years later the last regular goods services to be operated by steam came to an end. In the meantime, the plan entitled 'The Reshaping of British Railways' was published in 1962, and as a consequence the route mileage of British Railways was reduced from over 17,000 miles (27,370 km) in the year of publication to under 12,000 miles (19,320 km) by 1970, while passenger stations were reduced from 743 to 299 over the same period.

The end of steam operation thus coincided with a drastic reduction in the number of branch lines and local passenger services, effecting a complete transformation of the railway scene in Britain. The wisdom of the abandonment of steam has been debated endlessly in economic, operational and political terms, but the most widespread appeal of the steam locomotive is undoubtedly emotional and aesthetic. In this respect, one bonus of the simultaneous abandonment of branch lines and steam locomotives has been the restoration and preservation of locomotives and complete railways by groups of enthusiasts.

One of the Fairlie double engines, first built in 1869, in service on the Ffestiniog Railway

One of the most historic of these preserved railways is the festiniog line in North Wales, originally opened in 1836 as a gravity and horse tramway serving slate quarries, and converted to steam operation in 1864. In 1870 the festiniog Railway began operating the new Fairlie type of locomotive, effectively a double engine with two boilers and two sets of driving wheels and a central firebox and driving platform.

The Fairlie's ability to operate on steep gradients and sharp curves stimulated the construction of narrow-gauge lines in many parts of the world, and although the locomotives did not prove satisfactory in most places the current operation of Fairlie types on the festiniog line forms a link with a fascinating period of steam railway history.

MODERN
EUROPEAN STEAM

STATE OWNERSHIP OF RAILWAYS began much earlier on the European continent than in Britain. Alongside the principal companies in France, for example – the Nord, Est, Midi, Oest, Paris-Orléans and Paris-Lyons-Mediterranée, which had been organized by the government to radiate from Paris – in 1878 the Etat, or state system, was formed from a group of small companies in the west of the country.

The result was to create a competitor for the Paris-Orléans on the route to Bordeaux, while the Midi's control of the routes to Spain meant that the PO's services were in rivalry with those of the other connecting line, the PLM. With this stimulus, the Orléans built up the fastest trains in the country in the late nineteenth century, and in 1907, for its difficult main line to Toulouse, it introduced the first engines of the Pacific type in Europe.

These were four-cylinder de Glehn compounds, and a second series with superheaters was followed by a third with bigger driving wheels for the higher-speed services on the Bordeaux line. The compound system developed by Alfred de Glehn and his partner Gaston du Bousquet used a pair of high-pressure cylinders outside to drive the second pair of coupled wheels, and a low-pressure pair inside acting on the leading axle. The system was used widely in France and elsewhere in Europe, though in Britain, where George Churchward tested some French compound Atlantics, the additional complication of compounds never found wide acceptance, and the Pacifics introduced on the PO influenced other railways to follow suit.

Among the most prestigious of the French services were the Nord boat trains that formed the connection between Calais and Boulogne and Paris. In 1910 du Bousquet had been working on a 4–8–4 design for the Nord, but his death put an end to the development, and the company was forced to adopt Pacifics of a type developed by de Glehn for the Alsace-Lorraine railway.

Previously, du Bousquet had designed for the Nord company a 4–6–0 with relatively small wheels and enlarged steam passages to give the necessary higher piston speeds. After the First World War, the Nord planned a new class of 'Super-Pacifics' using the larger steam passages developed for the 4–6–0. The first example had been designed by George Asselin in 1914, only for their production to be delayed by the war, but after their introduction in 1923 they proved capable of extremely heavy work. The last batch, the Collin 'Super-Pacifics' introduced in 1931, were able to maintain 60-mph (96·6-kmh) schedules with the 500-ton (508-tonne) boat trains between Paris and the Channel ports.

While these engines were being built for the Nord, one of the greatest of all locomotive designers had started work in the research department of the Paris-Orléans company. This was André Chapelon, who concentrated his efforts on improving the circulation of the steam. To this end he introduced internal

streamlining of the steam passages, and increased the temperature in the superheaters to enable superheated steam to be fed to the low-pressure cylinders. At the same time, he adapted a device originated by the Finnish engineer Kylala for dividng the steam jet from the blast pipe to give improved draught on the fire without restricting the flow of the exhaust steam from the cylinders.

The results of these improvements, when applied to a PO Pacific, were an increase in power of 50 per cent, along with more economical use of fuel. Once

Previous page: A rebuilt 01·5 class Pacific of the Deutches Reichsbahn climbs towards Honebach tunnel with the Paris-Magdeburg express in

Below: No 3570, one of the third series of Paris-Orléans superheated compound Pacifics with the Paris restaurant car express at Tours

the details became known, other French railways either bought new or rebuilt PO locomotives that were being made redundant by electrification, or applied Chapelon principles to their own designs. By 1938, when the various companies were absorbed into the Société National des Chemins de Fer (national railway company), Chapelon's influence was dominant, though it was some years before he succeeded to the office of engineer-in-chief.

The development of improved types was interrupted by the outbreak of the Second World War, the German invasion of June 1940 coinciding with the completion of the prototype 160A.1, a 2–12–0 freight engine. This remarkable engine incorporated four low-pressure cylinders, with the steam being re-superheated after leaving the high-pressure pair, and steam jackets for the cylinders which might well have made superheating unnecessary.

However, this and other Chapelon prototypes and proposals were eclipsed by the decision to end the production and use of steam on the French railways, and the post-war locomotives produced were gen-

Inset, top: The arrival of the inaugural Golden Arrow boat train service between Paris and London at Calais in September 1926, with a Nord Pacific at its head

Inset, bottom: The Collin 'Super-Pacific' No 1253 at the head of the Golden Arrow in the forests of Chantilly near Paris in 1935

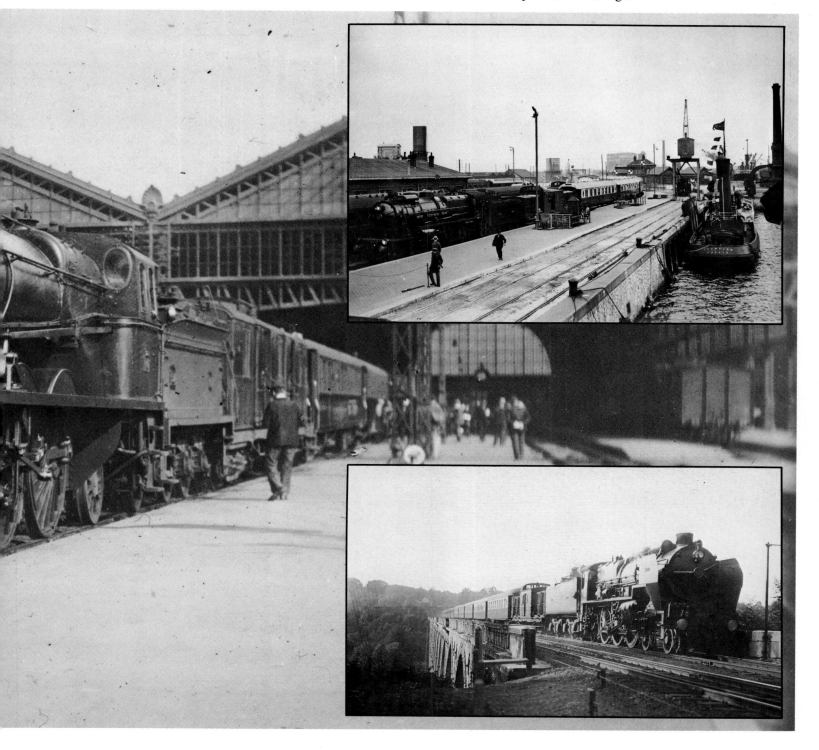

erally spin-offs from earlier designs that did not represent the height of development, but rather the most readily available adaptations of older models. Thus, the 241P 4–8–2s were based on a pre-war PLM type, while the 232U 4–6–4s were based on a wartime design.

In Germany, both state-owned and private railways had been built from the beginning, and the formation of the German federation in 1917 was followed by the gradual absorption of the private

Below: The class 232U four-cylinder compound 4–6–4 was first produced for the French national railway system in 1949

Right: SNCF 4–8–2 No 241P.10 with the Thermal Express at Vierzon in June 1967, after taking over from electric traction for the journey to Clermont Ferand

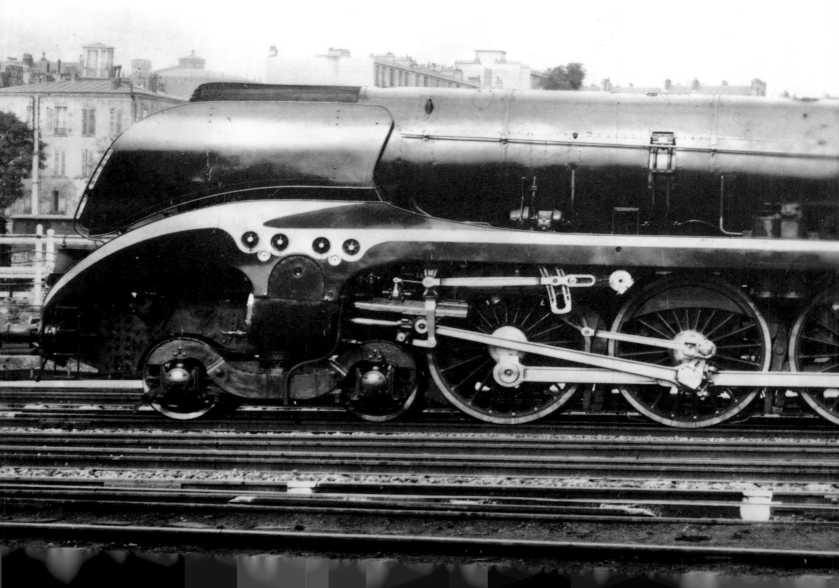

Right: No 241P.33 leaves Angers with a Paris-Nantes express, while a class 141R runs into the station with a local train for Le Mans in June 1967. The class 241P engines were first built in the late 1940s, and were derived from a pre-war design of the Paris-Lyons-Mediterranee railway

lines into the state systems. The dominant member of the federation was Prussia, and after the First World War the majority of the locomotives built for the new Reichsbahn (state railway) were of Prussian types.

However, the south German states of Bavaria, Baden and Württemberg had produced many distinctive designs, and the Bavarian railway had pioneered the use of 4–6–0 and Pacific types for express passenger trains. The Bavarian S3/6 class Pacific, introduced in 1908, was the only non-Prussian type to be built for the Reichsbahn after its formation. They were constructed by the firm of Maffei, and were used on the fastest German trains, including the famous Rheingold express along the Rhine valley.

Of course, the great German contribution to steam locomotive design was the superheating system developed by Wilhelm Schmidt in the late 1890s. The purpose of superheating was to raise the temperature of the steam well above that produced in the boiler so that after expanding in the cylinders it would still be hot enough to avoid the condensation that occurred otherwise.

Various attempts were made to achieve the necessary extra degree of heating, but it was Schmidt's firetube system that superseded all others. Steam from the boiler was collected in a header in the smokebox, then led through enlarged firetubes, or flues, by narrow pipes, which doubled back to a second compartment in the header, whence it was fed to the cylinders.

The Prussian state railways were among the first to adopt the new device, which enabled compound operation to be dispensed with. Another benefit was that the superheated steam was able to do more work than the ordinary saturated steam, so that boiler pressures could be reduced and larger cylinders used instead, leading to a considerable reduction in maintenance requirements.

The most famous Prussian product of this period was the P8 class 4–6–0, of which some 3,850 were built, 3,370 going to the Prussian state railway alone. They remained in service for many years, and after the First World War were used by several other countries which received them as part of the war reparations Germany was forced to make after the Armistice.

In the period between the wars, Richard Wagner was responsible for the new locomotive designs for the Reichsbahn, and among his products was the O1 class Pacific, which, along with the later O3, became a standard type. The 231 examples of the O1 series were the principal passenger express locomotives of the period, though the typical low pressures and two-cylinder simple machinery meant they were not the fastest of engines, compensation for this fact coming from their durability.

After the Second World War, both the name and many of the locomotives of the Deutsches Reichsbahn were taken over by the German Democratic Republic, and a number of O1s were rebuilt with bigger boilers, Boxpok wheels, Giesl ejectors (see below) and other modifications.

Another of Wagner's designs that remained at the prototype stage was the streamlined O5 class 4–6–4. The first of two examples was completed in March 1935, and one subsequently reached a speed of 124 mph (199·6 kmh) on level track, a performance which compares favourably with the *Mallard*'s downhill record of 126 mph (202·9 kmh).

Right: A German P8 class 4–6–0 at Eutingen in May 1969

Below right: A P8 at Trier engine shed in March 1967. The first P8 was produced for the Prussian state railways in 1906, and a final total of 3,850 were built. Many were used by other countries after the First World War, when steam locomotives were among the reparations which Germany was forced to make under the terms of the Armistice

Below: A class S3/6 Pacific, built by Maffei for the Bavarian state railways from 1908, and the only non-Prussian design to be built for the Reichsbahn after the First World War

Right : The prototype class
05 streamlined 4–6–4 No
05.001 with its builders in
March 1935. One of the two
engines of this type reached
a speed of 124 mph (199·6
kmh) on level track

Below : A rebuilt class 01
Pacific of the Deutches
Reichsbahn leaves Kulm-
bach with the Hof-Bambers
express in March 1972

Sharing frontiers with both France and Germany, the Alpine republic of Switzerland has developed one of the most varied railway systems in the world. Although Switzerland would not appear to be the most likely candidate for an extensive railway network, one of the first acts of the new government formed by the country's federation in 1848 was to ask Robert Stephenson to advise on the creation of a national railway system, and Swiss railways today are easily the busiest in Europe.

As far as power is concerned, electrification began early in the twentieth century, and was completed on the state system in 1960, but in the meantime some interesting steam operations were mounted. On the main lines there were high-speed services on the valley routes, while before being electrified in 1922 the line through the Gotthard Tunnel, originally the independent Jura-Simplon line, demanded extremely powerful engines.

Perhaps most fascinating, however, are the narrow-gauge and rack systems used to reach the less accessible points on the railway map. In 1858, for the opening of the Hauenstein line, which climbs 600 ft (182·9 m) in 6¼ miles (10·1 km) between Sissach and Laufelfingen, the locomotive *Genf* was employed to haul the official train. The unusual system used to give increased adhesion was developed by the Austrian engineer Engerth for use on the Semmering Pass, and involved carrying the frames of the tender ahead of the locomotive firebox, and using gears to drive the front pair of coupled tender wheels. The Swiss central railway used as many as 60 similar locomotives during the later years of the nineteenth century.

The Swiss railway system inevitably involved many impressive tunnels and bridges, while narrow-gauge lines were common and rack railways came into their own. One railway which combined all four was the metre-gauge Furka-Oberalp, with a rack system over the steepest sections and an impressive viaduct leading to the Gringiols spiral tunnel. This line, too, has been electrified.

The last rack railway to be operated by steam was the Brienz-Rothorn line, which climbs over 5,500 ft (1,676·4 m) from the shores of Lake Brienz to the summit of the Rothorn. A striking feature of the rack locomotives, which engage a rack laid between the running rails with a cog wheel to obtain traction, and which always operate downhill of the cars, is their canted bodies. These enable them to remain roughly horizontal on the steepest sections and prevent the forward part of the firetubes from being exposed by water running to the back of the boiler. Early rack locomotives often had vertical boilers for the same reason.

Another country which has more than its fair share of mountains is Switzerland's eastern neighbour, Austria, centre of a Balkan empire before the First World War rejigged the map of Europe. Both private and state railways were built in the nineteenth century,

Left: Locomotives Nos 2 and 4 on the Brienz-Rothorn line, the last regular steam-operated rack railway in Switzerland

Right: Class HG 3/4 2–6–0 of the Furka-Oberalp railway crosses the Grengiols viaduct at the entrance to the spiral tunnel with a special excursion from Brig to Obervald in May 1967

Below: The 0–4–6T Engerth type locomotive *Genf*, built in 1858, heads a special train from Sissach to Laufelfingen in August 1978 in celebration of 120 years of the Hauenstein line

and strategic requirements dictated the location of many of the long-distance routes that connected with the railways of neighbouring countries. One of these was the line from Vienna to Trieste that included the famous Semmering Pass section, which involves several miles of heavy gradients, and where a series of trials were held in 1850 to find a suitable form of locomotive for working the route.

Many services involved the negotiation of steep, sharply curving lines, and the compound locomotives of Karl Gölsdorf which predominated on Austrian railways at the turn of the century were based on the compound system. Gölsdorf's own refinement of the compound method was the introduction of an arrangement of steam inlets that passed steam directly to the low-pressure cylinders for starting or low-speed working, switching automatically to compound operation as the cut-off of the steam was shortened.

Gölsdorf was also a great innovator in the matter of wheel arrangements, producing the first 2–6–2 engines in Europe and the first 2–6–4 and 2–12–0 types to appear anywhere, specializing in models with large numbers of driving wheels in a wheelbase flexible enough for the sharp curves. One of the most popular types for heavy work in the conditions encountered on the difficult Austrian lines was the 4–8–0, and the class 33 locomotives produced after Gölsdorf's death were able to handle curves of less than 400-ft (121·9-m) radius.

Another Austrian innovator was Dr Giesl-Gieslingen, who in the 1920s developed a form of exhaust ejector using a fan-shaped array of steam jets which, carefully calculated to suit the particular locomotive and with a characteristic elliptical chimney, gave much greater efficiency. It was not until the 1950s that Giesl was able to interest the state railways in his device, but when it was tried it was found to give fuel savings of up to 25 per cent, and large numbers of Austrian locomotives were fitted with the device in the 1950s to improve their efficiency.

Right: A steam locomotive on the Abt system rack railway to the summit of the 5,400 ft (1,646 m) Scharfberg in Austria

Below: Austrian state railways class 33 4–8–0, a type first produced in 1923, near Brietenstein on the Semmering railway in 1955, after modification with the Giesl exhaust ejector. This device gave a considerable improvement in fuel economy

Italy is another European country where the original railways were built by individual states, and where electrification began at an early stage. It was only in 1870 that the unification of Italy was achieved, and the old state systems continued to operate until after the First World War.

Perhaps the best known fact about Italian railways is that Mussolini made the trains run on time, though this is actually as much a myth as might be expected. The credit actually belongs to Carlo Crova, who in the 1920s was responsible, as general manager of the new state system, for the old Adriatic, Mediterranean and Sicilian systems, and who succeeded in imposing order and punctuality on them: the fascists happened to be handily placed at the time to take the credit.

Among the locomotives that have operated on Italian railways are some unusual designs. In 1900 the Plancher type with the cab in front of the boiler

was built to make life easier for the crew in the narrow tunnels of the Adriatic main line, and in 1937 another cab-in-front design was produced by Attilio Franco, whose concern was with improving boiler efficiency. Franco's ideas were developed by Piero Crosti into a distinctive type of boiler which carried feed water tanks alongside the main boiler, and led the exhaust gases through these to chimneys at the sides of the boiler.

This boiler was used on a series of 83 modified locomotives of the 743 class, among other Italian types, and was used on ten of the British BR9 standard type 2–10–0s. As with other innovations of this period, however, it appeared too late for a full evaluation of its worth, though the extra complication of construction and maintenance would probably outweigh the savings of 10 per cent in fuel, except where coal was in short supply.

Above: A class 242F oil-fired 4–8–4 engine of the Spanish state railways with a Miranda-Zaragoza express in September 1969.

Left: An Italian class Gr 743 2–8–0 locomotive, one one of a series built from 1954 with the Crosti system of pre-heaters on the sides of the main boiler

Right: A Mikado type 2–8–2 engine of the Spanish state railways class 141F with a freight train

Left: A Swedish passenger
train leaves Ockelbo station
in the early 1920s, with a
B class 4–6–0 at its head

Below: One of the standard
freight engines on the broad-
gauge Finnish railway
system, a Tr I class 2–8–2 at
Helsinki in 1968

All the railways systems discussed so far have been of standard gauge, at least on the main lines, but there are two areas of Europe where a different gauge was chosen. One of these is the Iberian peninsula, where Spanish and Portuguese railways use a gauge of 5 ft 6 in (167·6 cm). Spanish railways were initially built by both the various states and by private concerns, using imported locomotives. After the First World War, however, most Spanish locomotives were built there, and in 1941 the railways were nationalized.

Conditions on Spanish railways are often similar to those in Austria, with long-distance routes and many mountain sections, and the 4–8–0 was adopted at an early stage. Subsequent designs have typically had eight-coupled driving wheels, with two or four leading and trailing wheels. A distinctive example is the F2001 class 4–8–4, a big and powerful type first

built in 1955 and used to operate heavy passenger services.

The other European broad-gauge railway system is at the opposite end of the continent, where Finnish and Russian railways are built to the 5 ft (152·4 cm) gauge. Finland has only about 3,000 miles (4,830 km) of route, and a correspondingly small number of locomotives, though steam locomotives continue in service. The two main classes are the Hr 1 Pacifics, for passenger traffic, and the Tr 1 2–8–2s for freight services.

Elsewhere in Scandinavia, the availability of hydro-electric power has led to electrification replacing steam, though in Sweden at one time numerous independent companies operated alongside the state system, and the variety of locomotive types was enormous.

INDIAN AND
PACIFIC STEAM

INDIAN STEAM RAILWAYS began in the 1850s, with a gauge of 5 ft 6 in (167·6 cm). This was chosen by the Governor-General of the day, Lord Dalhousie, on the basis of the evidence presented to the investigating committee considering the two gauges being used in Britain: it was intended to obtain the advantages of a broader gauge than the Stephenson Standard, without going to the extreme of Brunel's 7-ft (213·4-cm) track.

The difficulties of construction in India, and the urgent need for more lines, led to consideration of building narrow-gauge feeders, and in 1870, on the basis of the size of carriage needed for horses and artillery, Lord Mayo, another Governor-General, selected 3 ft 3 in (approximately 1 metre). So two 'standard' gauge networks were built, termed broad and metre gauge respectively, and with the subsequent addition of many narrow-gauge lines – that is, narrower than the metre gauge – India came to have one of the most varied railway systems in the world. Currently, as many as ten million passengers a day are carried on Indian trains, and while electrification is being carried out as rapidly as economic circumstances permit, much of the operation is still by steam.

Shortly after independence was achieved in 1947 – and with it the partition of the country and the separation of the railway system into Indian and Pakistani administrations – the introduction of new standard classes of locomotives was begun. The Pacific type had been selected by the Locomotive

Previous page: One of the standard broad gauge Pacifics of the Indian state railways, the WP class, arrives at Agra Cant station at the head of the Toofan express in December 1974

Below left: A metre gauge YP Pacific at Hubli with a local train to Dharwood in December 1981

Below: A WP Pacific at the head of a passenger train passes one of the equivalent standard freight engines, a WG 2–8–2, at Phulwari Sharif, near Patna

Below right: A broad gauge 2–8–2 at Agra Fort station in December 1974

Standard Committee in the 1920s as permitting large fireboxes and grates suitable for low grades of coal, and light, intermediate and heavy designs of classes XA, XB and XC were produced for the broad gauge lines. Corresponding YB Pacifics and ZB 2–6–2s were evolved for the metre and narrow gauge lines, while for freight work XD and even bigger XE 2–8–2s for the broad gauge and smaller YD and ZE 2–8–2s for the other gauges completed the range.

The Second World War saw the arrival of numbers of American locomotives supplied under Lend-Lease, and the first examples of the new standard design of Pacifics, the WP class, were ordered from Baldwin in the United States. Ultimately, a total of 755 WPs were built in a number of foreign countries as well as

in India. The freight counterpart of the WP was the WG 2–8–2, and as with the earlier classes there were metre gauge YP and YG equivalents. Again, indigenous production was supplemented by large orders from other countries, and the total of WGs alone reached 2,450.

Although the basic designs have been standardized, the locomotives themselves are given an attractively exotic appearance by the individual embellishment of the engines, while the tenders and smoke deflectors are painted in the appropriate colour indicating the zone in which it operates. The nine different zones were established after independence to facilitate administration after the railways were brought under state control.

For all the achievements of the builders of the 40,000 mile (64,000-km) Indian railway network, and of the administrators in running a transport system for so many people, the most famous of all India's railways is a little 2-ft (61-cm) gauge line that twists its way from Siliguri up into the foothills of the Himalayas and the old hill station of Darjeeling.

The line was begun in 1879, and in reaching its destination at a height of 7,400 ft (2255·5 m) the line goes through five zig-zags and four spirals, not in tunnels but on the open hillside. Consequently, the Himalayan scenery provides more than adequate compensation for the seven hours that are spent in completing the 55-mile (88·6-km) climb.

The locomotives used on the Darjeeling line are of an 0–4–0T saddle tank design first built in 1879, five years after the opening of the railway. The newest date from 1927, and of the total of 30 that were procured at intervals most are still operational.

Until 1937, the Indian railway system extended into Burma, which before that date was administered as a province of the Indian Empire, but the metre gauge Burma Railway never made any connection with the railways of its eastern neighbour, Thailand. These were standard gauge when construction began in the 1890s, but were converted after the First World War to conform with the metre gauge adopted by the southern railway when the latter was built south to a connection with the Malayan state system.

The various lines of the Thai railways radiate out from Bangkok, reaching the borders of Laos and Cambodia, and the locomotives used were imported from various foreign builders, including Britain, the United States and Japan. Since the early 1960s, when diesels took over passenger services, steam has been gradually eliminated, but while it was used the two most obvious characteristics of the locomotives were their clean appearance and use of wood for fuel.

The normal intention of colonial administrations in building railways was as a means of either extending control of the territory or exploiting its natural resources. In the latter case, railways were not necessarily public carriers: one of the most widespread applications of narrow gauge steam railways was in sugar plantations, where a lightly laid track would enable a small locomotive to collect wagons loaded with the cane, often collected on temporary feeder lines by animal traction.

An example of this practice, combined with a public railway, occurred on the islands of Fiji. Grants made to the Colonial Sugar Corporation to enable it to cultivate plantations of sugar cane were made conditional on the company operating a free passenger railway, and little 4–4–0 locomotives, built by the British firm of Hudswell-Clarke and of a type commonly used for light industrial and agricultural work, operated the passenger service on a 2-ft (61-cm) gauge track. These were replaced by diesel engines.

Right: Hudswell-Clarke 4–4–0 on the free passenger railway operated on the south Pacific islands of Fiji in conjunction with the sugar cane plantation railways

Below right: One of the last steam-hauled trains in Thailand, an immaculately clean American 2–8–0 with a freight train near Bangkok

Below: No 792, one of the 0–4–0 saddle tank engines used on the Darjeeling-Himalayan railway

At the other end of the scale of steam railway operation is the Chinese state system. In the nineteenth century, the Imperial government resisted railways as they did the other innovations of the western powers which attempted to colonize parts of the country. Railways were built more or less as military superiority allowed, and the years of anti-western uprisings, civil war, Japanese occupation and more civil war that occupied most of the first half of the twentieth century meant that railway construction did not begin in earnest until the establishment of the communist government in 1949.

Consequently, Chinese railways are still being built on a large scale, and much of the operation continues to be by steam. Since the initial programme was begun with Soviet technical assistance, the locomotives show strong Soviet influence. The QJ class 'Forward' 2–10–2 heavy freight engines, for example, first built in 1956 and in continued construction in modernized form since 1964, bear a strong resemblance to the contemporary Soviet LV class, though scaled down from the Soviet 5-ft (152·4-cm) gauge to the standard gauge used in China.

One distinctive feature inherited from the Soviet designs is the prominent casing on top of the boiler which encloses a steam pipe leading forward from the dome to a regulator box which is sited on the smoke-box behind the chimney. This casing is also apparent on the JS 2–8–2 'Liberation' and RM 4–6–2 'People' classes. Like Indian locomotives, the Chinese engines display an attractive variety of ornamentation and decoration.

Opposite: Front view of a Chinese QJ 'Forward' class 2–10–2 heavy freight engine, based on the Soviet LV class and in production since 1956

Below: A 1951-vintage 4–6–4 tank engine of the Queensland Railways with a passenger special crosses a viaduct on a zig-zag railway in January 1978

In the south Pacific, steam railways in Australia and New Zealand are now in the hands of the many preservation organizations, diesel and electric traction having taken over main-line operations.

The Australian railways were slow to develop in the early stages. A sparse population, concentrated in widely dispersed centres, and separate colonial administrations in six different regions, led to initial building of more or less local lines. More seriously, an early agreement between Victoria, South Australia and New South Wales to adopt a gauge of 5 ft 3 in (160 cm) was broken by New South Wales, which changed to standard gauge: the other two states, having already ordered broad gauge locomotives, went ahead with the agreed measure, so that when the first railways were opened in the 1850s there were two different gauges in use.

The situation become more complicated during the 1860s and 1870s, when the other states began building their first railways. Tasmania followed Victoria and South Australia in using the 5 ft 3 in (160 cm) gauge, but Queensland and Western Australia went for economy of construction with yet a third gauge, this time of 3 ft 6 in (106·7 cm), which was later applied to the Tasmanian system and to some lines built in South Australia.

The consequence of all this variety in gauges was that Victoria and South Australia were the only two states with a common border and the same gauge of railway. Moreover, full advantage was taken of the narrow gauge's opportunity for light track, relatively sharp grades and tight curves, so that subsequent

Left: One of the preserved
Ab class Pacifics of the
New Zealand Railways
near Lumsden in January
1978

Far left: Bb class 4–8–0
with a mixed train on the
Wilton line crosses Fore-
wood Creek viaduct

Below: An Ab class Pacific
at the head of the Kingston
Flyer special service
operated between Lumsden
and Kingston

Bottom: Preserved Z17 class
locomotive and C20 tank
engine at the head of an
Australian special passenger
service

development was restricted by the track within states as well as by the guage changes between them.

The immense variety of locomotives that appeared, as imported models were supplemented by the various states' own production, is well represented by the numerous museums and preservation societies, and the same is true of New Zealand, where agreement over gauges hindered early building of railways.

Ultimately, New Zealand standardized on a gauge of 3 ft 6 in (106·7 cm), and all lines were of this gauge by the end of the 1870s. The locomotives of this period were predominantly tank types, but in 1874 the first J class 'Canterbury Goods' 2–6–0 tender engines were built. A total of 32 of these were acquired, and the last was not withdrawn from service until 1955.

The J class, like all locomotives used up to this period, were imported from England, but in 1878 the first indigenous types appeared. In the early years of the twentieth century typical products included the B, Ba and Bb 4–8–0 goods engines, of which a total of 50 were built, the majority being the Bb type for passenger and mixed as well as goods services.

In 1906 one of the most successful of all New Zealand steam locomotive designs appeared in the shape of the A class Pacific, a four-cylinder compound on the de Glehn system. A total of 57 were built, and after a long career on the express services, some were still at work on coal trains when steam was finally superseded by diesel power on the west coast coal lines in 1969.

When further examples were required in 1914, the outbreak of the First World War meant British builders were unable to accept any orders, and a series of 10 4–6–2s, designated tue Aa class, were obtained from Baldwins in the United States. A more significant type, however, was the Ab class, of the following year, which used superheating to dispense with the A class compound operation, and featured the novel Vanderbilt type of tender, which incorporated a cylindrical water tank. A total of 141 were built, mostly in New Zealand, with further examples supplies by the North British Locomotive company.

Later New Zealand types included the K class 4–8–4, designed to be the most powerful locomotive possible given the rather restricted loading gauge on the New Zealand lines. The 30 original Ks were supplemented by the improved Ka class, and the Kb type which added a booster unit for use on the most heavily graded sections on the South Island.

For the lighter rails used on secondary lines, the J class 4–8–2s appeared in 1939. In their original form the J class were given an impressive style of streamlined casing, though this was later removed, and the later Ja class omitted it altogether. These were the last steam locomotives designed for New Zealand Railways, as the conversion to diesel operation began in 1948 with the first orders for diesel shunting engines, the first main-line diesels following two years later.

STEAM IN AFRICA

THE GEOGRAPHICAL AND POLITICAL difficulties that have attended the building of railways in Africa have prevented the evolution of anything like a comprehensive network. Generally, railways have been built for specific purposes, usually to enable the products of inland mines to be carried to the coasts, and to minimize the cost and difficulty they have been built to metre or 3 ft 6 in (106·7 cm) gauges.

At one stage the colonist Cecil Rhodes had ambitions to build a railway from the Cape of Good Hope to Cairo, uniting the various British colonies and colsolidating the British administration from Egypt to South Africa. This grandiose scheme ignored both the rivalry between the various colonial powers and the sheer scale of the physical barriers.

The latter were encountered in full measure by the builders of the Uganda Railway, begun from Mombasa in 1896, and which was forced to climb a series of escarpments, culminating in the 8,327 ft (2,538 m) Mau summit, before reaching its goal of Lake Victoria. Although built to the 3 ft 6 in (106·7 cm) gauge, the Uganda Railway was ultimately converted to metre gauge and formed the basis for the East African Railway connecting Uganda and the Kenyan capital of Nairobi with the port of Mombasa.

In order to obtain sufficient power for working the heavy trains made necessary by the predominantly single-track, narrow gauge lines with restricted loading gauges, articulation was resorted to at an early stage, and of the modern types of articulated locomotive, the Mallet type that was developed so successfully in North America was the first to be used. However, the Mallet system, which mounts a large boiler on two powered bogies, while permitting curves to be negotiated readily, demands a long and cumbersome boiler and, especially in its original compound form, resulted in locomotives of great complexity.

Early in the twentieth century, an Australian engineer, Herbert Garrat, developed a new system of articulation, which involves mounting the water tank and fuel bunker on separate engine units fore and aft of the boiler which is carried between the two. As well as allowing the locomotive to pivot at two points, the Garrat system has a number of other advantages. A high adhesion weight is spread over a long wheelbase, a large diameter of boiler can be used, and the firebox grate can be deep and wide, since there are no wheels and axles underneath to limit its size.

The Garrats were developed by the British firm of Beyer-Peacock, and the Beyer-Garrat locomotive proved ideal for African conditions immediately it was introduced in South Africa shortly after the First World War. On East African Railways the biggest

Previous page, top: One
of the Beyer-Garrat
articulated locomotives of
the former Rhodesian
Railways with a coal train
near Boabab in May 1976

Previous page, bottom:
A 59th class Beyer-Garrat
4–8–2 + 2–8–4 on the metre
gauge East African Railways
en route from Nairobi to
Mombasa in January 1971

Right: One of the non-
condensing models of the
South African Railways 25
class 4–8–4 locomotives with
a mixed goods train near
Spyfontein in April 1979

of all Garrats were introduced in 1955 in the form of the 59 class, the most powerful metre gauge locomotives to be built for any railway, which were capable of handling 1,200 ton (1,220 tonne) freight trains on the climb from Mombasa to Nairobi. The 59 class have the wheel arrangement 4–8–2 + 2–8–4: earlier classes pioneered the 4–8–4 + 4–8–4 arrangement for use on lighter sections of track.

The former Rhodesian Railways were also great users of Garrats. More amenable terrain allowed generally higher speeds to be reached with passenger services, and some of the fastest Garrat types were used, though their introduction also allowed an enormous increase in the volume of freight handled.

The Rhodesian railways were originally an extension of the Cape Province system, and as such were built to the Cape gauge of 3 ft 6 in (106·7 cm). While it was on South African railways that the Beyer-Garrat first proved its ability, and the type has seen extensive use in the republic since the 1920s, most locomotives used there were of more conventional design.

To compensate for the rather slow speeds of passenger trains, a notable line in luxury trains was developed in South Africa, epitomized by the famous Blue Train. This service between Cape Town and Johannesburg had its origin in the Union Limited, established in 1903 to connect with the arrival of the Union Castle mail ship from England.

In keeping with this tradition, a special excursion has been mounted by the Railway Society of Souther Africa and using luxury sleeping, dining and lounge cars hauled by a selection of steam locomotives. A ten-day round trip through the spectacular scenery of South Africa in the most luxurious of accommodation makes this one of the ultimate railway excursions.

Another tradition which South African railways have maintained is that of innovation in steam locomotive development. Two examples of this were designed to cope with the long stretches of main line through arid country where there was a need for very powerful engines.

The first, built by the North British Locomotive company from 1953, was the class 25 4–8–4 with condensing tender. A total of 90 engines were built, along with 50 non-condensing equivalents, and the condensing engines are able to travel the remarkable distance of 700 miles (1,127 km) without taking water.

The other dates from 1955, and is a Beyer-Garrat design, the GMAM 4–8–2 + 2–8–4, which achieves its objective of covering long distances on relatively lightweight track by using an auxiliary water tank holding 6,750 gallons (30713 litres) of water. One of the most notable aspects of this design is the construction of the first example in only seven months from the placing of the order. Conversion to diesel traction on the majority of the African railways, however, meant that the GMAM was one of the last classes of Beyer-Peacock locomotives based on Garrat's design.

STEAM IN AMERICA

By THE END OF the nineteenth century passenger trains on the railway network of the United States were notable more for the distance they covered than for their speed. Well over 150,000 miles (241,500 km) had been added to the 30,000 miles (48,300 km) of route that existed fifty years before, and this astonishing rate of construction could only have been achieved on the accepted principle of laying the track to the minimum standard necessary to get the trains running, and bringing it up to a more satisfactory level with the resulting revenues.

The recurring financial panics and associated bankruptcies of large numbers of railroads that punctuated the nineteenth century were an indication of the chronic insolvency of many railway operations. Often the interest payments on bonds issued to finance initial construction proved such a crippling burden that there never was any money for track improvement; maintenance was neglected; and it became simply impossible to run fast trains without risking derailments.

Of course, this was not true of all railroads. In the north-east of the country, the route between Chicago and New York had become one of the busiest and most important with the completion of the trans-continental railroad and Chicago's emergence as the focal point for westward travel, and a number of railroads were engaged in fierce competition to provide the fastest services. The two main competitors were the New York Central, with the water level route up the Hudson and round the shores of the Great Lakes, and the Pennsylvania Railroad, whose route was some 56 miles (90·2 km) shorter, but which included some arduous mountain sections.

One peak of competition was reached in 1893, the year of the Columbian Exposition in Chicago, when 44 through trains a day were scheduled over a total of 18 different routes. The New York Central's premier service was the Empire State Express, advertized as the fastest train in the world, and operated by some of the biggest engines of the American Standard 4–4–0 type ever built.

These were the work of the railroad's locomotive superintendent, William Buchanan, who had begun by rebuilding existing 4–4–0s with bigger fireboxes and higher pressure boilers. Having taken this line of development as far as he could with the conventional position of the firebox between the driving wheel axles, Buchanan produced a new design in which the firebox was raised above the frames. The result was a most singular appearance, with the boiler pitched very high, but one of the new models, No 999, was timed at 90 mph (145 kmh) on a test run, and went on

Previous page: The famous New York Central No 999 4–4–0, which claimed a record speed of 112½ mph (181·1 kmh) with the Empire State Express in 1893, preserved at Chicago

Top left: A Missouri Pacific 4–6–4 heads the Sunshine Special through the Arcadia Valley in Missouri in 1920

Top centre: A Northern Pacific passenger train leaves Desmet, Montana in 1939

Top right: L2 Hudson No 307 of the Chesapeake and Ohio Railway prepares to leave Cincinnati with the *George Washington* in the 1940s

Centre left: The Great Northern Railway's *Empire Builder* leaves St Paul on its inaugural run to Seattle on 11 June 1929

Bottom left: The chicago and North Western Railway's 400 leaves Chicago in the 1930s

Bottom right: An EM-1 Mallet articulated loco-motive with a coal train at the highest point of the Baltimore and Ohio Rail-road's main line system near Altamont, Maryland

81

to make the best times with the Empire State Limited.

The climax of No 999's career came in May 1893, when it was claimed that the Empire State had covered a mile (1·61 km) in only 32 seconds, equal to a speed of $112\frac{1}{2}$ mph (181·1 kmh). This was so far in advance of anything achieved elsewhere that the timing was regarded with some suspicion, which appeared to be confirmed when the maximum speed attained in an official attempt to break the British record established in the course of the 1895 race to Aberdeen was a more realistic 81 mph (130·4 kmh). Nevertheless, No 999 was preserved, though only after the special 7 ft 2 in (218·4 cm) driving wheels used on the high-speed runs to Chicago had been replaced by standard 5 ft 10 in (177·8 cm) examples, and another boiler fitted.

The necessity for changing at Chicago was a legacy of the origins of the transcontinental railway, which had been authorized by Congress to build west from the Missouri River at Omaha, Nebraska. The first railroad from the east to reach the opposite bank at Council Bluffs was the Chicago and North Western, and for some years this was the venue for an uncomfortable ferry across the river before the Union Pacific train could be boarded.

By the early part of the twentieth century there were a number of alternative routes to the west coast. By acquiring the Chicago, Burlington and Quincy Railroad, James J. Hill, owner of the Northern Pacific and Great Northern roads, was able to complete the route from Chicago to Seattle and Portland over which the appropriately named Empire Builder service was inaugurated in 1929.

During the 1930s many newly named trains were introduced in an effort to stem the loss of passengers that resulted from the growing use of private cars and the economic depression that followed the stock market collapse of 1929. By that time the Chicago and North Western and Union Pacific had eradicated the bottleneck at Omaha by cooperating to run the City of San Francisco and City of Los Angeles to California, while the City of Portland and City of Denver served their respective cities, the latter service connecting with the Denver and Rio Grande Western's California Zephyr.

None of these services did anything to eradicate the need for a change at Chicago, and during the 1930s competition between the New York Central and Pennsylvania railroads was as fierce as ever. The respective prestige services on the two lines at that time were the Twentieth Century Limited and Broadway Limited. In 1910 the Pennsylvania had opened its new station in the centre of New York, so that intending passengers no longer had to take a ferry from Manhattan Island to Jersey City before beginning their journey, and by the 1930s both railroads were running their fastest trains to Chicago in only 16 hours.

Travellers on these trains had to pay for the privilege. An agreement between the various railroads offering services between the two cities had established a standard time of 28 hours, and a supplementary charge for every hour by which this was reduced. Since the Twentieth Century Limited and Broadway Limited were first class only, with another additional charge for the Pullman service, fares were well over double the ordinary price.

In return, the passengers were provided with some of the most luxurious trains ever operated. Bathing

One of the New York Central's celebrated 4–6–4 Hudsons heads west through the water troughs at Dunkirk, New York, in March 1952

facilities, with a choice of fresh or salt water, gourmet food, a barber shop and, for those who had time to work, secretaries and telephones were among the inducements offered, and specially designed streamlined trains symbolized the nature of the services.

Naturally, such luxury made for very heavy trains, and the combination of high speeds and great weight demanded fast and powerful locomotives. Both the New York Central and the Pennsylvania had a long tradition of outstanding locomotive design, and some of their finest types were used on the Chicago service.

In the early twentieth century, the New York Central's fastest passenger engines were of the Pacific type, the culmination of the series being the K5 class introduced in 1925. Having reached the limit of development with Pacifics, the company went on to develop an entirely new type, the 4–6–4, which became known from the location of its main line as the Hudson.

Starting with the J1 class of 1927, the New York Central developed its ultimate type, the J3, by 1937. The latter were capable of reaching 95 mph (153 kmh) with trains weighing more than a 1,000 tons (1,016 tonnes), and its total of 275 Hudsons outnumbered the 4–6–4s of all other US railroads put together.

The Pennsylvania had also developed a notable series of Pacifics, beginning with the K2 class of 1907 and culminating in the K4 class introduced in 1914. But by that stage the Pennsylvania had begun a process of electrification which was extended during the 1920s to cover all its lines from the subsidiary Long Island Railroad in the north to Washington, DC, and west to Harrisburg, Pennsylvania. Possibly because the eventual aim was to electrify more of its lines, there was no successor to the K4, which remained in service as a result until 1942.

When it came, the replacement for the K4 was an unconventional design of 4–4–4–4, not an articulated design, but an extremely large engine with two pairs of outside cylinders driving two sets of coupled wheels.

Below left: A J class 4–8–4 of the Norfolk and Western Railroad with the Southern Railways Tennessean on N&W tracks near Elliston, Virginia en route from Lynchburg to Bristol

Below: A Union Pacific 4–8–4 with a northbound passenger train at Denver, Colorado, in July 1952

These did not prove as successful as early designs, however, and the Pennsylvania was soon to go over to diesel traction.

Meanwhile, the New York Central had continued its process of development, producing the 4–8–4 Niagara type, which was specifically designed to match the greater availability that was one of the diesel locomotive's great attractions. Unfortunately, cracks in the special boilers brought their careers to an early end, but only after the six used on the New York-Chicago route had recorded an average mileage of over 300,000 miles (483,000 km) in their first year.

Another railway which made a similar effort to maximize the efficiency of its steam locomotives was the Norfolk and Western. Being a major carrier of coal from the West Virginia coalfields, the Norfolk and Western had something of a vested interest in prolonging the use of steam. Accordingly, the railroad's design staff designed a range of new locomotives, of which the J class 4–8–4 was the express

passenger type.

With a handsome streamlined casing, altogether more businesslike in appearance than some of the more extravagant examples used by other railroads, the J class were designed for maximum reliability and ease of maintenance. They were also the most powerful of all American 4–8–4s, as well as among the fastest, and were able to move 1,000-ton (1,016-tonne) trains at 80 mph (129 mph), despite having rather small driving wheels, and on a test run on straight track the impressive speed of 110 mph (177·1 kmh) was reached with a train weighing 1,000 tons (1,016 tonnes).

Perhaps more important, they were also capable of long periods of work with only short intervals for servicing, and their average mileage of 15,000 miles (241,150 km) per month was particularly notable in view of the fact that the main passenger line, between Norfolk and Cincinnati, was under 650 miles (1,046·5 km) long.

Bottom left: One of the famous K4 Pacifics of the Pennsylvania Railroad westbound at Mount Union, Pennsylvania, in September 1952

Below: One of the biggest of all steam locomotives, Union Pacific 4–8–8–4 Big Boy No 4002

Above left: Union Pacific Big Boy No 4019 with a string of fruit cars in Echo Canyon, Utah

Below: Union Pacific 4–8–4 No 4488 with a southbound Klamath train at Dunsmuir, California, in June 1952

Left: Union Pacific 4–8–4 No 829 heads out of a depot with a passenger train

Above: Big Boy No 4004
preserved at Cheyenne,
Wyoming

Below: A streamlined E4
class 4–6–4 of the Chicago
and North Western Railway
in the 1940s

Ultimately, the Norfolk and Western was forced to abandon steam in the face of wholesale adoption of the diesel on American railways. Although it built its own locomotives at its shops at Roanoke, Virginia, maintaining what would soon become an anachronistic steam operation became increasingly difficult, and during the late 1950s steam was finally abandoned.

Another railroad which used 4–8–4s for its express passenger services was the Union Pacific, which has a long tradition of using the biggest locomotives. The first Union Pacific 4–8–4s were introduced in 1937 for high-speed services over the original transcontinental route between Cheyenne and Ogden, and the last steam locomotive built for the railroad, 4–8–4 No 8444, has been preserved in working order.

Another type introduced for the Cheyenne-Ogden section was the famous Union Pacific Big Boy 4–8–8–4 Mallet articulated locomotive. The biggest steam locomotives ever built, the Big Boys weighed 540 tons (549 tonnes) and were 132 ft (40·2 m) long overall. Among the tasks for which they were designed was running express fruit trains over the Wasatch mountains between Ogden and Green River, where the 4–6–6–4 Challengers took over for the other mountain section to Cheyenne.

The Union Pacific also has a line south to Denver, which in the 1870s became the centre of a famous system of narrow-gauge lines. At one stage there were armed battles between employees of this railroad, the Denver and Rio Grande, and those of rival lines, but ultimately the narrow gauge was abandoned, and Denver became a focal point for a number of wester railroads.

However, two sections of the old narrow gauge, between Durango and Silverton and from Antonito to Chama, continue to be operated as steam tourist railways, the former under the name of the Cumbres and Toltec Scenic Railroad.

Above: A double-headed
train nears the summit of
the Cumbres and Toltec
tourist railway, part of the
old Denver and Rio Grande
narrow gauge system

Right: Union Pacific 4–8–4
No 8444 with a steam special
between Denver and Sterling
in October 1979

Below: One of the Canadian Pacific's compound 4–4–2s with a Montreal-Ottawa fast passenger train leaves Westmount station around the turn of the century

Bottom: The Canadian Pacific's Dominion transcontinental service headed by a Selkirk type 2–10–4 alongside the Bow River in the Canadian Rockies in 1945

The transcontinental railroad's opening up of the western United States in the 1870s was mirrored in the following decade by the building of the Canadian Pacific. The construction of a transcontinental railway in Canada was actually embodied in the agreement by which the former independent colony of British Columbia became part of the Canadian federation in 1871. The original stipulation was that the line should be completed within ten years, though it was another 15 years before the first trains were running between Montreal and the Pacific coast.

This was a formidable achievement, however, in view of the succession of mountain ranges in the west and the combination of rock and swamp with which the builders had to contend in their progress round the north of Lake Superior. After reaching the brink of bankruptcy during construction of the railroad and surviving a difficult period in its early years, the Canadian Pacific Railway grew to become one of the most successful rail operations in North America.

The other principal component of the Canadian railway system is Canadian National, which was formed after the First World War from a combination of government-owned lines and bankrupt private enterprise systems. The competition between the two main systems has helped promote some excellent services on Canadian railways, and some outstanding locomotive designs.

Early locomotives were generally of the American 4–4–0 type, and for the services between Montreal and Ottawa Canadian Pacific produced a design of the Atlantic type 4–4–2 in 1899. These were four-cylinder compound engines, and they were able to operate 48-mph (77·3-kmh) services, including intermediate stops, between the two cities.

The dominant problem in Canadian railway operations, however, has always been the western mountain ranges. The steep climbs to the mountain passes placed severe strains on the locomotives working these sections. To deal with the climb through the

A preserved example of the Canadian Pacific Railway's celebrated Royal Hudson 4–6–4s

Kicking Horse Pass route, Canadian Pacific in 1829 produced the first of its famous class of 2–10–4 Selkirks.

Transcontinental trains had operated over the Canadian Pacific since its first year, and unlike their counterparts in the United States, Canadians could travel all the way from the principal cities of the east to the shores of the Pacific on the same train. The Canadian Pacific transcontinental service, the Do-

minion, was taken from Calgary west over the Rocky and Selkirk mountains from which the type derived its name by these big and powerful engines, which were equally at home heading heavy freight trains.

Contemporary with the Selkirks were the most famous of all Canadian locomotives, the Hudsons. These were 4–6–4 passenger engines produced by the Montreal Locomotive Works, the same firm that built the Selkirks, and they were at their most impressive

on the Montreal-Ottawa services, where they worked some of the fastest schedules in the world in the 1930s.

The first batch of 20 Hudsons were followed by a further 30 built in 1937, and after one of the later models had headed the royal train in which King George VI toured Canada in 1939, the second series engines were given crowns on the running board skirts either side of the smokebox, becoming known as the Royal Hudsons. Other distinguishing features of the later models were the domeless boiler and semi-streamlined appearance.

Although steam working on Canadian railways had been phased out by 1960, a number of Royal Hudsons have been preserved. One of these, No 2860, was maintained in operating condition by the British Columbia government, and used to haul excursion trains between North Vancouver and Squamish on the British Columbia Railways.

In South America the railway systems share some of the characteristics of those in Africa, having been started by foreign promoters – largely British and American – using a mixture of gauges, and tending to carry natural resources from inland sources to coastal ports, and to link the most important cities in the coastal areas.

The railways of Argentina were operated by predominantly British companies until nationalization in 1949: at that point they were in need of large-scale modernization, and the position was not made easier by the existence of three separate gauges, the broad gauge of 5 ft 6 in (167·6 cm), standard gauge and metre gauge, with additional lines of narrower gauges.

An example of the narrow gauge operations is provided by the 250-mile (402·5-km) branch line from Ingeniero Jacobacci to Esquel. Built to the 2 ft 6 in (76·2 cm) gauge and operated by steam, this line has many of the characteristics of the rural railway, with slow, mixed trains serving the needs of a sparsely populated area.

A contrast with the Argentine operation is offered by the line through the Bolivian Andes from Rio Mulato to Potosi. At its highest point, this line reaches 15,705 ft (4,787 m) at Condor, barely 100 ft (30·5 m)

below the highest railway in the world, at La Cima in Peru. The style of service is similar, however: a weekly mixed freight and passenger train hauled by a 2–8–2 locomotive on a metre gauge track.

It is fitting to end in Peru, for it was here that Richard Trevithick, the man who started it all, turned up in 1816 on his gold mining expedition. He proposed a railway over the 9½ miles (15·3 km) between Lima and the port of Callao, but the wars of independence of the early nineteenth century prevented the realization of this scheme until 1851, by which time Trevithick had returned to England and died.

The line from Lima to Callao eventually formed part of the Central Railway of Peru, which includes the high point of Cima. The other Peruvian railway, also standard gauge, is the Southern, and among the motive power on this line were oil-burning Baldwin 4–6–0s which provided a daily passenger service.

Of course, to characterize all South American railways as quaint rural and mountain survivals from another age would be wrong. They serve as a reminder of the remarkable ability of the steam train to go almost anywhere it is wanted, to operate in the most unlikely circumstances and the most rugged of environments, and to achieve tasks that were impossible by any other means for over a century.

Opposite: Oil-burning Baldwin 4–6–0 No 100 leaves Machu Picchu station with the passenger train to Cuzco on the Peruvian Southern Railway in the Andes

Below: A mixed train on the Rio Mulato-Potosi line in the Bolivian Andes

INDEX

The publishers would like to thank the following individuals and organisations who supplied illustrations for this book.
For reasons of space alone, some references have been abbreviated as follows:
Baltimore & Ohio Railroad = B&O
R Bastin = RB
BBC Hulton Picture Library = BBC
Burlington Northern Railroad = BN
Canadian Pacific Railroad = CP
Chicago & North Western Railway = CNW
D Cross = DC
C Gammell = CG
J Jarvis = JJ
Mechanical Archive & Research Services, London = MARS
National Railway Museum, York = NRM
B Stephenson = BS
Union Pacific Railroad Museum, Nebraska = UP
J Winkley = JW

Front cover: A Orchard. Back cover: V Goldberg. 2–3 JJ. 4–5: BBC. 6–7: National Coal Board. 8–9 (top): Science Museum. 9: CG. 10–11 (top): B&O. 10–11 (btm): NRM. 11: B&O. 12: CG. 12–13: Mary Evans Picture Library. 12–13: JW. 14–15: NRM. 16: JW. 16–17: NRM. 17: MARS. 18 (top): CG. 18 (btm): Ironbridge Gorge Museum. 18–21: RB. 22: US National Archives. 23: MARS. 24–25: Peter Newark's Western Americana. 26: JW. 26–27: JW. 27: Peter Newark's Western Americana. 30: JW. 34–35: DC. 36: NRM. 36–37: DC. 38 (top & centre): DC. 38 (btm): JW. 39: DC. 40 (top): DC. 40–41: BS. 42: JW. 42–43: DC. 44–45: JW. 46–47: BS. 48–49: Vie du Rail. 49 (btm): BBC. 50–51: SNCF. 52: Krauss Maffei AG. 53 (top): CG. 53 (btm): RB. 54–55: BS. 55: Bundesarchiv. 56: DC. 56–57: BS. 58: A Luft. 59: Austrian State Railways. 60: Italian State Railways. 60–61: Colour-rail/JG Dewing. 61: RENFE. 62: Swedish State Railways. 62–63: Finnish State Railways/Mikko Alatieri. 64–65: CG. 66–68: CG. 69: DC. 70–71: CG. 72 (top left): DC; (top right): CG. 72–73: New Zealand Government Railways. 73: J Dunn. 74–77: CG. 78–79: JW. 80 (top): Missouri Pacific RR. 80 (centre): BN. 80 (btm): CNW. 80–81 (top): MARS. 80–81 (btm): B&O. 81: CNW. 82–84: JJ. 85–86: UP. 86–87: JJ. 87 (top): JW. 87 (btm): CNW. 88: CG. 89–91: Canadian Pacific. 92–93: K Mills.

The Eastbound Grand Canyon Limited out of Los Angeles headed by a 4–8–4 Sante Fe 3765 class locomotive in Cajon Pass, California